MW01531796

"Who is A Disciple of Christ?"

To A Wonderful person and a special friend

"Who is A Disciple of Christ?"

John Graham

Copyright © 2009 by John Graham.

ISBN: Hardcover   978-1-4415-7438-1
             Softcover   978-1-4415-7437-4

All rights reserved. No part of this book may be reproduced or transmitted in any
form or by any means, electronic or mechanical, including photocopying, recording,
or by any information storage and retrieval system, without permission in writing
from the copyright owner.

This book was printed in the United States of America.

To order additional copies of this book, contact:
Xlibris Corporation
1-888-795-4274
www.Xlibris.com
Orders@Xlibris.com
67956

CONTENTS

CHAPTER ONE

"He Is A Listener!"

The first thought that comes to mind when I hear the term "disciple" is someone who has disciplined themselves to learn a certain philosophy or someone who had devoted themselves to walk a certain path. While this definition may be somewhat true, I believe that a disciple must first hear the call "to follow".

I read once, that we may be doing Jesus an injustice in stressing the fact that He so frequently said "Go . . . !" His first word to His disciples was not "Go" but "Come."

I believe this answers in part the question, "Why are there not more disciples of Jesus?" With all the distractions and different avenues one can take in life, very few take time to listen for the call of Jesus. God told stubborn Israel "you have neither heard nor understood" (Isaiah 48:8 NIV).

God wired humanity with an internal system called a soul. God made man "a living soul" according to Genesis 2:7 and 1 Corinthians 15:47. Humanity became a living being with the ability to hear and heed the call of God. Yet, man has been caught up in the whirlwind of activities and worldly allegiances. Therefore, in stubbornness or self-centeredness, man refuses to hear the call to the discipleship of Jesus.

Some individuals have misconceptions regarding the call issued by God. Therefore, they turn a deaf ear to God. They distance themselves from hearing range (or so they think). They clutter their minds with ungodliness. "God made man upright, but men have gone in search of many schemes" (Ecclesiastes 7:29 NIV). Humanity has invested their life in things unprofitable and invented things of no benefit.

Until we are willing to listen and allow our spirit to lead us toward the direction of Christ, we will never have fulfillment. Our spirit will be restless, seeking relief from discontentment and difficulties of life. "In which you used to live when you followed the ways of this world and of the ruler of the kingdom of the air, the spirit who is now at work in those who are disobedient. All of us also lived among them at one time, gratifying the cravings of our sinful nature and following its desires and thoughts" (Ephesians 2:2-3 NIV)

We are caught in the crossfire between righteousness and rebellion, godliness and godlessness, spiritual life and sin, deed to eternal life and death. To tune God in or turn God off is dependent on our willingness to listen.

No one can become a disciple of Jesus Christ unless he first hears the call "to follow." "Faith comes by hearing the message, and the message comes by the Word of Christ" (Romans 10:17 NIV). Discipleship begins when we receive in our head the tender and true call of Jesus, then response from our heart in honest and humble commitment.

The Greek word for "to follow after" occurs 90 times in the New Testament. This term most often denotes the action of someone answering the call of Jesus. The term refers to at least the initial stages of conviction and commitment. Most consider the invitation of Jesus to "follow Me' as an invitation to salvation.

In Matthew's account of the Gospel (chapter 4), we see Jesus called to Simon and Andrew, James and John, to leave their worldly commitments and willingly commit to following Him. Later in chapter 9, Jesus calls Matthew. And in chapter ten we read these words "And when he had called unto him his twelve disciples: Peter, Andrew, James, John, Philip, Bartholomew, Thomas, Matthew, James, Thaddeus, Simon, and Judas." This was the beginning of the ministry and mission of Jesus Christ to make disciples.

In Revelations, John records the words of the Lord, "Here I am! I stand at the door and knock. If anyone hears My voice and opens the door, I will come in" (Revelations 3:20 NIV). Jesus will not bang down the door of your life to set up residence; but with kindness and keen awareness of your need to know Him make his wish known.

He knows you need Him and He wants you. Yet it is your choice. You must listen to His loving call and life-giving desire to fellowship with you and have you to follow Him—the only way to happiness, hope and heaven. Jesus answered, I am the way and the truth and the life" (John 14:6 NIV).

I have often heard that men have selective hearing. That is, according to women, they hear what they want to hear. And this may be true in many cases. However, how true is it in regard to all mankind, male and female, listening and legitimately hearing what God has to say? Do we hear what we want to hear or do we hear what we think is best for us.

In fact, I think sometimes, we hear the call of God and even respond without really realizing the cost involved. When we are faced with the choices of obeying Christ or enjoying the opportunities of pleasure of this world, we follow selfish desires.

Just as Jesus called with authority the first disciples and they responded without hesitation; He has expected no less from every generation since that first century. He personally knocks at the door of your life and without fanfare, invites you to walk in the life, light and liberty which He has to offer. "In (Christ) was life; and the life was the light (for) man" (John 1:9 KJV).

Without hearing and heeding the call of Jesus, we have neither lasting short-range purpose nor long-range goal. "Godliness is profitable unto all things, having promise of the life that now is, and of that which is to come" (I Timothy 4:8 KJV).

The call of God is one of enrichment, enjoyment and everlasting life. No other party, person, or philosophy will grant us this combination of blessings and benefits.

Roy Robertson listed "seven hearing aids" that is very important in listening to the call of God or in the continual conversation a disciple may have with God on a daily basis. They were:

(1) Listen reverently ("Quiet everyone—a holy silence. Listen!"—Habakkuk 2:20 Message).
(2) Listen expectantly ("everything I hope for comes form him, so why not [listen]"—Psalm 62:5 Message).
(3) Listen prayerfully ("Samuel answered, 'Speak. I'm your servant, ready to listen."—1 Samuel 3:10Message).
(4) Listen attentively ("Then all the multitude kept silence, and gave audience"—Acts 15:12 KJV).
(5) Listen understandingly ("They read from the Book of the Law of God, making it clear, and giving meaning so that the people understand what was being read"—Nehemiah 8:8 NIV).

(6) Listen discerningly ("they received the Word with all readiness of mind"—Acts 17:11KJV).

(7) Listen obediently ("Knowing the correct pass word isn't going to get you anywhere with me. What is required is serious obedience"—Matthew 7:21 Message).

It is important to train oneself to listen. You'll be amazed at what you can learn when your mouth is shut.

Not everyone will hear and heed the call of Jesus. In Luke, chapter nine, we read where Jesus called three different individuals to follow him, yet each made an excuse and desired to be exempted.

When He calls, Jesus desires man to respond. If man would only consider what blessings were in store for him in following Jesus and become His disciple.

Let me end this chapter with a unique story. A young and successful executive was traveling down a neighborhood street, going a bit too fast in his new Jaguar. He was watching for kids darting out form between parked cars and slowed down when he thought he saw something. As his car passed, no children appeared. Instead, a brick smashed into the Jag's side door! He slammed on the brakes and backed the Jag back to the spot where the brick had been thrown. The angry driver then jumped out of the car, grabbed the nearest kid and pushed him up against a parked car shouting, "What was that all about and who are you? Just what the heck are you doing? That's a new car and that brick you threw is going to cost a lot of money. Why did you do it?"

The young boy was apologetic. "Please, mister . . . please, I'm sorry but I didn't know what else to do." He pleaded, "I threw the brick because no one else would stop, with tears dripping down his face and off his chin, the youth pointed to a spot just around a parked care. "It's my brother," he said. "He rolled off the curb and fell out of his wheelchair and I can't lift him up."

Now sobbing, the boy asked the stunned executive, "Would you please help me get him back into his wheelchair? He's hurt and he's too heavy for me."

Moved beyond words, the driver tried to swallow the rapidly swelling lump in his throat. He hurriedly lifted the handicapped boy back into the wheelchair, then took out a linen handkerchief and dabbed at the fresh scrapes and cuts. A quick look told him everything was going to be okay. "Thank you and may God bless you," the grateful child told the stranger. Too shook up for words, the man simply watched the boy push his wheelchair-bound brother down the sidewalk toward their home.

It was a long time, slow walk back to the Jaguar. The damage was very noticeable, but the driver never bothered to repair the dented side door. He kept the dent there to remind him of this message: "Don't go through life so fast that someone has to throw a brick at you to get your attention!" God whispers in our souls and speaks to our hearts. Sometimes when we don't have time to listen, He has to throw a brick at us. It's our choice to listen or not.

CHAPTER TWO

"He Is A Loser"

Immediately, upon reading this chapter title, some will began to think "what in the world goes here." Some may become somewhat turned off. But remember the first step to discipleship is he is a listener. So, hear me out.

On each occasion when Jesus called his disciples, they were busy doing certain things. Some were fixing tears in their fishing nets, others were fervently working on various projects, and one fellow was sitting at his position as tax collector. Jesus issued his call "to follow Him" and they immediately left all to follow. "James and John, the sons of Zebedee, which were partners with Simon . . . when they had brought their ships to land; they forsook all, and followed him" (Luke 5:10-11).

Now Jesus needed disciples, who once trained, would become apostles, "send ones." However, the principle of leaving their present priorities to take on a new priority is still applicable today. "If any man will come after me, let him deny himself; and take up his cross and follow me" (Matthew 16:24 KJV). We must come to Jesus on His terms. He is all we need, therefore, let us hear him and be willing to sacrifice and surrender all to know Him.

A disciple of Christ is one that gives himself to be wholly at Christ's disposing; to become what He teaches, to believe what He reveals, to boldly obey what He commands, to break from what He forbids, to bear what is inflicted by or for Him, in expectation of that reward which He has promised.

In fact, I am convinced that one who desires to be a disciple of Christ is one who would rather lose all they have in the world, and suffer all that an enraged world can inflict on them; than deny the relationship and responsibilities of a disciple.

"Then Peter said, lo, we have left all, and followed thee. And (Jesus) said unto them, Verily I say unto you, There is no man that hath left house, or parents, or brethren, or wife, or children, for the kingdom of God's sake, who shall not receive manifold more in this present time, and in the world to come life everlasting" (Luke 18:29-30 KJV).

Now, I do not believe that Jesus ever intends for us to break off our family relationships during our time on earth. However, I do believe that we must set priorities. We must let loose those people, projects and possessions that take up our time of devotion and dedication to Jesus Christ. We must surrender our time, talents, and treasures to Him.

Maybe "loser" is a bad word to use in this instance; although the Apostle Paul stated, "I consider everything a loss compared to the surpassing greatness of knowing Christ Jesus my Lord" (Philippians 3:8 NIV). Remember the words of the Lord to the twelve disciples, "Anyone who loves his father or mother more than me is not worthy of me; anyone who loves his son or daughter more than me is not worthy of me; and anyone who does not take his cross and follow me is not worthy of me. Whosever finds his life will lose it, and whoever loses his life for my sake will find it" (Matthew 10:37-39).

Jesus does not want to be a piece of the puzzle of your life; He desires to be your life. Because of the significance of our relationship with Christ, all things must revolve around Him and reflect His character. That is the plan of God, but it is also for the benefit of us. "But seek first his kingdom and his righteousness, and all these things will be given to you as well" (Matthew 6:33 NIV).

To give up something for Jesus is to gain something from Jesus. The Apostle Paul declared, "For I have lost all things. I consider these rubbish, that I may gain Christ and be found in him . . . I want to know Christ and the power of his resurrection and the fellowship of sharing in his sufferings, becoming like him in his death" (Philippians 3:8, 10 NIV).

Although the Apostle Paul, formerly Saul of Tarsus, had pride, position, possession and proper education; he did not have Christ. He had ambitions and aims in life. Yet, he counted all these secondary when it came to hearing the call from Christ and having to make a decision in following Him.

Becoming a loser of this world's goods should be the proper and precise thing to do when we consider that we did not create ourselves nor can we change ourselves. Yes, we may declare that we are self-made and that we have reformed our ways. But we have no absolute control over these decisions without the aid of God's Spirit and God's Scriptures.

Resolutions are broken in a month while regeneration can last a life time. Self-sufficiency soon becomes fragmented and fails. Therefore, it seems to be to our advantage to become a loser in order to become a winner. "For what shall it profit a man, if he shall gain the whole world, and lose his own soul? Or what shall a man give in exchange for his soul?" (Mark 8:36 KJV).

No one can be a disciple unless he is content to forsake all and follow Him. An individual must have such a strong affection to Christ as to hate all other things and have the willingness to give complete ownership to Christ. If this is not an agreement between you and Christ, then you may be only a pretender rather than a personal disciple of the Lord's.

It would be a dishonor and be displeasing to God to hear His call, and then be unwilling to evaluate your relations in life.

I am sure you have heard the expression, "I would give my right arm for it." Many have exchanged a lot of things for temporal blessings that soon faded away. Yet, God offers us an everlasting blessing that will not corrode, become corrupt, crack, nor cease to exist. It is an everyday relationship with Him. It is redemption from a life of sin that separated us from an abundant life. However, we must be willing to give everything to Jesus—our thoughts, our time, our treasure, our talents, our troubles, our talk, our transgressions, our thirst for the things of this life, our terrors (fears) and our trust.

Before we can take the third step of discipleship, which is being a learner; we must empty ourselves of those things that would hinder. It is only as we become a loser of a self-motivated lifestyle that we can be filled with the Word of God, the Will of God, the Way of God and the Work of God.

It was only as Peter became empty of self that he became filled and fit for the Spirit. He became a true disciple and spiritual director of the First Church in Jerusalem only after he discharged the spirit of individualism (pride) and impatience and dedicated himself to a complete overhaul by the spiritual creator—Jesus Christ.

"God's readiness to give and forgive is now public. Salvation's available for everyone! We're being shown how to turn our backs on a godless, indulgent life, and how to take on a God-filled, God-honoring life. This new life is starting right now, and is whetting our appetites for the glorious day when our great God and Savior, Jesus Christ, appears. He offered himself as a sacrifice to free us form a dark, rebellious life into this good, pure life, making us a people he can be proud of, energetic in goodness" (Titus 2:12-14 Message).

It may be necessary to sever relationships with certain individuals, stand against temptations that so easily beset us and surrender strongholds in our lives to Jesus. In losing these kinds of things, we gain more positive, purer and promising character than we could ever borrow, buy or build in this world.

CHAPTER THREE

"He Is A Learner"

The word disciple, translated from the Greek noun, is found 264 times in the Gospels and Acts. The noun has the basic meaning of "a pupil, apprentice, and adherent." The verb form occurs four times in the Gospels and once in Acts. It means to "be or become a pupil." Therefore, a disciple of Jesus is one who learns from the example and exhortation of Jesus Christ. He is one who declares a personal allegiance to the image (the person) and the inspiration (the principles) of Christ.

R. W. Hugh Jones once declared, "We have learned to fly through the air like birds and to swim through the sea like fish. When will we learn to walk the earth like men?"

We have built machines to move mountains and maneuver to the moon and Mars. We constantly design and develop preventive measures and materials against disease and devastating environmental upheavals. Yet, when will we decide to devote our life to the Creator.

The Greek term for disciple is found only in the Gospels and Book of Acts, as many as 264 times. Basically, the term refers to someone who attaches themselves to someone for the purpose of learning, with a view to committing themselves to what the person says.

Patrick Morley in his book, *What is a Disciple?*, defines a disciple as "someone called to walk with Christ, equipped to live like Christ, and sent to work for Christ." A disciple is one who learns from and one who lives the character of Christ.

Jesus said, "Come to me, all you who are weary and burdened, and I will give you rest. Take my yoke upon you and learn from me, for I am gentle and humble in heart, and you will find rest for your souls" (Matthew 11:28-29 NIV).

You see, every disciple is a believer, but every believer is not a disciple. To be His disciple is to yield to His will for our life and to be yoked with Him. A true believer will desire and devote himself to learn how to respond and how to relate to other individuals in life. In the Parable of the Good Samaritan (Luke 10), we see three individuals who were believers, yet they failed to prove discipleship. One felt he had a reasonable excuse, another did not feel it was his responsibility to react, while the true disciple reacted by going the extra mile.

Some believers are curious, some are convinced, while others are committed. Which do you think Jesus desires? It is good to be curious, but let us become convinced and committed.

He invites us to come unto Him, let loose of all the emotional and evil baggage of our life and learns the new and noble way of living. He came to delivery humanity from the shame, sorrow and suffering that sin produces. "Who hath delivered us from the power of darkness, and hath translated us into the kingdom of His dear Son" (Colossians 1:13).

He invites us to learn how He made it possible to be freed from the passion, pride and penalty of self-righteousness. "Being made free from sin, ye became the servants of righteousness" Romans 6:18 KJV).

He invites us to learn how He will give power to overcome the temptations, traps, and tricks of Satan. "The Lord will rescue me from every evil attack and will bring me safely to his heavenly kingdom" (2 Timothy 4:18 NIV).

He invites us to learn how He can give you a new life filled with His love, His life and His liberty. "Stand fast in the liberty wherein Christ hath made us free" (Galatians 5:1 KJV).

He invites us to learn how He can use every life to "salt" the earth, "shine" His glory and "show" His love to all humanity. "Now when they saw the boldness of Peter and John, and perceived that they were unlearned and ignorant men, they marveled; and took knowledge of them, that they had been with Jesus" (Acts 4:13 KJV).

It will be no easy task to learn how to lean on and live the foundation and fundamentals that His Word will teach.

As we come unto Him, He will create a desire within us to know His wonderful words of life—The Bible. He says, "If you abide in My word, you are My disciples indeed"(John 8:31 KJV). The Psalmist declared, "Thy Word have I laid up in my heart, that I might not sin against You" (Psalm 119:11 AMP).

I am reminded of a cute but concrete thought regarding the Bible. A father was approached by his small son who told him proudly, "I know what the Bible means!" His father smiled and replied, "What do you mean, you know what the Bible means? The son replied, "I do know!" "Okay," said his father . . . "What does the Bible mean? "That's easy, Daddy . . ." the young boy replied excitedly," It stands for "*Basic Information Before Leaving Earth.*"

The more we learn from Christ and about Christ, the more we will overcome and the greater the opportunity to share Him. But we must become a pupil before we can perform the work of the Lord. Don't lose the energy or the enthusiasm; just prepare yourself by learning day by day in your devotion with God.

The world is getting tougher physically, tighter financially and more troubled emotionally. Therefore, we must gain internal strength and stability. Charles Crabtree, General Superintendent of the Assemblies of God, stated in the prologue of the book, D*eveloping Dynamic Disciples,* "it's not the outward pressures that determine a Christian's life, but it is the inward braces". Is not this what the Apostle Paul mean when he said, "the life that I live in the body, I live by faith in the Son of God" (Galatians 2:20 NIV).

The more we learn of the Word and from the Word, the greater the influence and the inspiration is available. The will, the wisdom, the walk of our life is stronger. Although we still will face trials, temptations and troubles; our load will become lighter, our light for Jesus will become brighter, and our liberty will become more stable.

Our devotion to God becomes stronger and sweeter as we enjoy and become enriched in His Word and as we enter into a time of waiting on Him and enjoying having words with Him. The disciples made this clear when they observed the practice of Jesus talking with the Father and openly seeing the benefits of such a relationship; then they asked, "Lord, teach us to pray" (Luke 11:1 KJV).

Prayer is daily communion with our Savior and Shepherd of life. It is an attitude and an action of sharing with the Lord and receiving from the Lord.

We learn to see things from God's perspective. We learn to build on God's promises. We learn to stand in God's power. As believers, we learn that we are blessed with "power, and of love, and of a sound mind" (2 Timothy 1:7 KJV).

Now, you must remember that you do not graduate from the school of hard knocks and heavenly learning in a few months, or years. It is a lifetime commitment. What we learn must become evident in our lifestyle. And our lives exist until the time of physical death or spiritual promotion—the rapture.

The disciples had responded to the call of Christ, cancelled their former lives and committed themselves to learn the new life. When Jesus was crucified, the disciples' world seemed to collapse. They were crushed. However, on three occasions Jesus came to them and had to remind them what he had taught them in order to revive their broken spirits—the disciples encounter with Jesus on the Emmaus road, the devotional breakfast challenge of Jesus on the shores of Galilee, and the doubt killing experience with Thomas behind closed doors.

As disciples, we must not let down our guard but grasp the hand of the Master and hold on for dear life—in courage, confidence and commitment. We must learn that He "will keep in perfect peace him whose mind is steadfast, because his trust is in (God)" (Isaiah 26:3).

James Allen once said, "Let a man radically alter his thoughts, and he will be astonished at the rapid transformation it will effect in the material conditions of his life." Is not this what the Apostle Paul meant when he said, "Do not conform, any longer to the pattern of this world, but be transformed by the renewing of your mind, then you will be able to test and approve what God's will is—his good, pleasing and perfect will" (Romans 12:2 NIV).

Once we learn the will of God for our lives, all other things become secondary and soon unimportant.

The called out ones who believed, should become pupils of the principles of God. He taught them about His amazing grace that embodied his full character of "love, joy, peace, patience, kindness, goodness, faithfulness, gentleness, and self-control" (Galatians 5:22-23 NIV). The fruit of the Spirit is the true character of life that every believer must accept and adapt in order to become His disciple. It is fruit that is produced when we become the branch of the True Vine (John 15).

Christ inspired teachings on the vices of the flesh (Galatians 5); as well as the virtues of the Spirit. His Word "teaches us say 'No' to ungodliness and worldly passions, and to live self-controlled, upright and godly lives" (Titus 2:12 NIV).

We must learn to think, to feel, and to act like He did. NO, it is not easy. No, it will not happen overnight or completely in this lifetime. But it is necessary to give Him our undivided attention to learn His Word, His will, and His way in order to do His work. And His work is walking daily demonstrating that we have been with Jesus.

A disciple of Christ learns what repentance, regeneration and restoration is and how it inspires and influences our life. We find it creates a new image and new ideals of living. "If we confess our sins, He is faithful and just to forgive us our sins and cleanse us from all unrighteousness" (1 John 1:9 KJV).

Repentance is an 'about face.' It is more than an announcement that 'I'm sorry'; it is a complete change of view with regard to sin. Repentance is our part in the plan of salvation. "Godly sorrow brings repentance that leads to salvation" (2 Corinthians 7:10 NIV).

Regeneration is God's part in the plan of salvation. It is the change He makes possible. He makes us a new creature. He changes us from the inside out. "Therefore, if anyone is in Christ, he is a new creation, the old has gone, and the new has come!" (2 Corinthians 5:17NIV).

Restoration is another word for the term "justification." Both means we have been acquitted, approved and accepted. We have been declared righteous. Our past is forgiven and forgotten. Our present is freshness and faithfulness. Our future is happiness and heaven.

Once we hear and heed the call to follow Christ; and once we lean on Christ to learn from Him; we began to focus and fervently seek Him—Not only in the study of His Word and the sincere communion with Him; but in our worship of Him in His House—the Church. The Bible declares, "Not forsaking the assembling of ourselves together . . . but exhorting one another (to be faithful to God's House)" (Hebrews 10:25 KJV (Emphasis). The Psalmist declared, "I was glad when they said unto me, Let us go into the house of the Lord" (Psalm 122:1).

It is in God's House where we learn how to fellowship with one another, fervently honor God by singing, sharing our finances, studying the Bible and shouting praises.

Learning is an ongoing process. It is an everyday experience.

Henry Ford said, "Anyone who stops learning is old whether this happens at twenty or eighty. Anyone who keeps on learning not only remains young but becomes constantly more valuable, regardless of physical capacity."

This is true of spiritual and scriptural learning. We must keep our head and heart filled with the knowledge of God. "Celebrate God all day, every day, I mean revel in him!

Summing it all up, friends, I'd say you'll do best by filling your minds and meditating on things true, noble, reputable, authentic, compelling, gracious—the best, not the worst; the beautiful, not the ugly; things to praise, not things to curse. Put into practice what you learned, what you heard, and saw and realized. Do that, and God, who makes everything work together, will work you into his most excellent harmonies" (Philippians 4: 4, 8-9 Message).

Little Johnny put it best when he stated after his first day of school. "I have to go back tomorrow because I haven't learned how to read or write."

Folks, there is always something else to acknowledge and acquire from God.

CHAPTER FOUR

"He Is A Leaner"

Throughout the Scriptures, we repeatedly are exposed to the term "trust." To trust is to "lean on, depend upon, have faith in." Solomon declared, "Trust in the Lord with all your heart and lean not on your own understanding" (Proverbs 3:5 NIV).

Leaning on Jesus is to acknowledge Him as your support and strength to maintain a meaningful life and to minister spiritual life as His disciple. From the very first day of our new life in Christ, we are like infants. We must begin living a new life all over again. Jesus told Nicodemus, "You must be born again" (John 3:6 NIV).

Therefore, as an infant depends on their parents for every personal, physical and psychological need; so must every new believer learn to lean on our spiritual guardian Jesus Christ. The writer of Hebrews stated, "ye have need that one teach you again which be the first principles of the oracles of God; and are become such as have need of milk" (Hebrews 5:12KJV).

The Apostle Paul stated, "I can do all things through Christ which gives me strength" (Philippians 4:13 NIV). The great Apostle also said, "And my God will meet all your needs according to his glorious riches (knowledge) in Christ Jesus"(Philippians 4:19 NIV). In fact, the last two chapters of Philippians, Paul points out the reality that our growth and gladness of life is based on our grateful acceptance of our total dependence on God.

Believers must depend on the "sincere milk of the Word of God," lean on the sheltering arms of the Master and place faith in the succoring presences of the Holy Spirit. In doing so; we become the disciple Jesus desires of us.

In chapter twenty-five of the book of Matthew, we find Jesus talking about the final judgment. Now, I am not going to deal with the subject that Jesus was dealing with, but I would like to draw your attention to the fact that if Jesus demands that as believers we do certain things in meeting social needs of individuals; how much more is he willing to supply these same needs in our lives. If we were to examine our lives we would find that it is He that we lean on to quench our thirsty and hunger ("trust in the Lord, and do good; so shall thou dwell in the land, and verily thou shall be fed"—Psalm 37:3 KJV), quicken our spirits ("thy Word hath quickened me"—Psalm 119:25 KJV) and quiet our fears ("Let not your hearts be troubled: ye believe in God"—John 14:1 KJV).

I remember when I was a child; I heard a story about a man who had a dream to travel across the country on a train. So, he saved up his money and purchased the ticket. After the ticket purchase, there was little money left. He decided to buy a few snacks to eat on his journey. As the days passed, he became very hungry. At one point of the journey he approached a porter and asked about the meals and how much they cost. The porter laughed, and told him, "Sir, the meals were included when you purchased the ticket."

Is this not like many believers? God provides a way for us to have a ticket to a happy and hopeful life. Finally, we accept the ticket to genuine life (see chapter two); however, we fail to lean on Christ for every benefit and blessing that comes with such an experience.

It is important to enjoy life and be enriched in life. Yet, it can only happen as we lean on Jesus twenty four/seven. He has promised to grant provisions, give power, and guide progressively.

"Blessed is the man (whose) delight (dependence) is in the law of the Lord and on his law, he meditates day and night. He is like a tree planted by streams of water, which yields its fruit in season and whose leaf does not wither. Whatever he does prospers" (Psalm 1:1-3 NIV).

It is to our benefit to lean on, trust in, have faith in and depend upon the Lord God. The Psalmist declared, "It is better to trust in the Lord than to put confidence in princes" (Psalm 118:9 KJV).

In this modern age of self-service gas pumps, I can still remember an old advertisement about an automobile service station. An ad that promised full service to your vehicle needs. The oil level was checked, the radiator water level was checked, the battery acid level was checked, the air in the ties were checked and adjusted to the right level, the windshield was cleaned and all done without expectation of a monetary tip. It was a slogan about Texaco. It said, "You can trust your car to the man who wears the star." It was a meaningful ad that promised genuine service regardless of who you were or what you drove.

Friends, I am convinced that you can trust your life to the One who made the stars. He will treat you with utmost courtesy and care and provide the courage and confidence to continue your journey. However, you must be willing to lean on Him, put your trust in Him, and depend on His availability and abilities.

As we learn to lean on Jesus, we find a sure foundation, a strong fortification and a sincere fellowship. I like what the great hymn, "Leaning on the Everlasting Arms" says. "What a fellowship, what a joy divine; what a blessedness, what a peace is mine. O how sweet to walk in this pilgrim way, O how bright the path grows from day to day. What have I to dread, what have I to bear, I have blessed peace with my Lord so near."

How displeased God must have been of the inhabitants of Jerusalem in the days of the prophet Micah. The presiding judges, the priest, and the people rebelled against God and ruled for their present prosperity. They took for granted the guardianship of the Lord.

Let us humble ourselves unto the Lord and become yoked with His will for our lives and we will be blessed. Micah asked, "yet will they lean upon the Lord" (Micah 3:11 KJV).

Friend, let us prove to be a true disciple of the Lord by recognizing our need of Him and relying on Him.

CHAPTER FIVE

"He Is A Lover"

Think with me for a moment. Jesus is in the upper room of a building in Jerusalem with His disciples. He has dined with them symbolizing his death as a sacrificial Lamb for their sins and their salvation. He has washed their feet symbolizing his devotion as a servant and His dedication to demonstrate true humility. Each of these participations were examples of His love for His disciples. Then He declares, "In the same way I love you, you love one another. This is how everyone will recognize that you are my disciples—when they see the love you have for one another" (John 13:34-35 Message).

No one can be a disciple of Jesus without desiring and developing the genuine love that Jesus has for mankind. We may never reach the depth or the height of His agape love, but we are to put forth every ounce of effort in attitude and action to love each other (in the church and outside the church).

In fact, Jesus responded to a scribe that questioned him regarding the greatest of the commandments with these words. "Love the Lord your God with all your passion and prayer and intelligence and energy, and loving others as well as you love yourselves" (Mark 12:30-31 Message). Remember: he loves not Christ at all who does not love Christ above all.

There is no doubting that man loves himself. We beautify our bodies; build our physique; buy garments that make us look nice; brace manners; and brag about who we are, what we have and where we have been.

And if this is true, and it is; then we must express and spare no expense in loving God and His prized creation, humanity.

I once read a short poem that went like this: "Love is a gift, take it, and let it grow. Love is a sign we should wear, let it show. Love is an act, do it, let it go. Love is a powerful element in our relationships of life. And if you really want to put it to the test, see what happens when it is applied to an enemy. Jesus did just that. Humanity was lost and living in sin, yet Jesus shed His life's blood and in doing so showered us with the drops of His great love.

Then the Spirit whispers the remission of the sin in one's life and shines forth the amazing love of God throughout our entire being causing an overflow of joy and jubilation. "God has poured out His love into our hearts by the Holy Ghost" (Romans5:5 NIV). God's love is without reservations and there is no respect of persons with God. Let us truly love as Jesus by not choosing who we love but simply love.

Thomas A Kempis once wrote, "If thou didst know the whole Bible by heart, and the sayings of all the philosophers, what would all that profit thee without the love of God, and without His grace? Vanity of vanities; all is vanity except to love God and to serve Him only."

There are books written on love. Books on family love relationships, friendships, female and male love experiences. C. S. Lewis penned a book entitled, *The Four Loves.* In it he distinguishes affection love, friendship love, Eros love, and charity love. He discusses the differences, the deceptions and distortions of all four loves. He lists the first three as "natural loves." The latter, charity, he refers to as the "sweetening grace of divine love."

To me charity is agape love in action and attitude. Agape love is "a total self giving love toward another." It is spiritual born love and sacrificial love. I read once a definition of agape love as "a gap eliminator." And my friend, this is the kind of love that God desires and demands of anyone who would become His disciple. It is a love that removes all hindrances and gives a residence to hope.

I feel it would be good for us to take a knee-deep examination of genuine, godly and scriptural grounded love as spoken of in the Apostle Paul's letter to the church at Corinth (1 Corinthians 13:1-13). By this, we mean to take a prayerful and purposeful look at these verses, and wade about knee deep into the thoughts to grasp a good meaning from them.

Jesus Christ was and is the supreme expression of the love of God ("For God so loved the world that He gave His only begotten Son"—John 3:16). His divine love and compassion is the gift of the Spirit to believers who will be yielded to Him ("And so we know and rely on the love God has for us. God is love. Whoever lives in love lives in God, and God in him"—1 John 4:22). To demonstrate scriptural and sacrificial love to walk and talk in a way that will not dishonor nor displease the One Who offers us His love.

Let us look at the characteristics of disciple defined love. It is "patient." To love patiently means "to endure or persevere." It is not easily broken or quick to give up. It will stand against the winds of adversity and be adventurous to mend and make up or conquer and complete. Are we willing to demonstrate this quality of character before Christ and the community?

A second quality of character of this love is "kindness." Since this term is connected with the first characteristic, maybe it is expressing a demonstrated patience with expressions that reinforces and reassures those to who we are having relations with. Oh, how we need expresses of kindness in daily activities and dealing with humanity.

A third characteristic is that this love "envies not." It other words, it is love that is filled and flowing with generosity, which is definitely an opposing concept to our modern society's beliefs. We live in a world filled with jealousy. Yet this discipleship love does not boil over with fits of jealousy. We must learn to possess the spirit of contentment, perform the task of assignment eagerly and pat others on the back when they are more successful doing the same work that we are attempting.

Another characteristic of discipleship love is it "is not boastful." It is not a love that builds on itself. It is a love that knows the foundation is God and if any bragging is to be done—it is praise to the Creator and Caretaker of our life—God. It is a love that develops discipline and devotion heaping praise on God and help toward others.

The next characteristic is very closely related to the previous one. It is a love that "is not conceited—arrogant and inflated with pride." Self-esteem is very important. Taking care of one self is necessary. In fact, the Scriptures declared "love your neighbor as yourself" (Mark 12:31 NIV). But to allow oneself to put forth a spirit of "I am something" or "I am better than you" or "just look what I have done" is definitely wrong and will discharge you from the ranks of a disciple. I know that our society is filled with slogans, signs, sounds and sights of self importance, but friend the love of God will never abide in the same chamber with pride.

Another closely related characteristic of discipleship love is that "it does not act unbecomingly or rude." This is a love in the little things of life—a demonstration of politeness and courtesy. In spite of a generation of people who desire instant gratification where virtues of civility and common courtesy falls in the street; we must share a smile, speak a word, stretch out a helping hand, slap someone on the back with congratulations or stand beside them when the world seems be crashing down around them.

What a lesson for everyone to review in this chapter of God's book! What principles of discipleship! What a challenge the love of God issues!

A seventh characteristic of disciple defined love is "it does not insist on its own rights or its own way; for it is not self-seeking." Simply put, it is a love that is known as unselfish. What a contradiction in our modern society where life is about "rights." Consumer rights, civil rights, child rights, criminal rights, constitutional rights; as well as, employment rights, environmental rights, educational rights and so forth. However, if we are to be a disciple of Christ, we must seek the things from above (truth, honesty, justice, purity, loveliness and good report) and not seek the rights that will shade or steal from our true purpose and priority of being a follower of Jesus. Keep in mind, once we yield our life to Christ, we need not worry about our worldly rights because God is in control of our life. And when He is in control and consumes our life with His love, we have more freedom than any legislated rights that is bartered, bought or begged for. As others behold our view of self-contentment and satisfaction in our relationship with God, they will be uplifted in spirit and in understanding of the importance of a spiritual relationship.

Looking still at this chapter, let us examine another of the terrific characteristics of discipleship love. It is love that is "not easily provoked." As a disciple, we must be one who is not easily ruffled, quick tempered, or of a touchy disposition. We must be one who takes no action of the evil done to us or one who makes no big deal out of suffering a wrong done to us personally.

Ouch, this challenges those of us who sometimes feel we are mature disciples. But one writer penned in references to this aspect of love by calling it "a sin of disposition." It is only as we fill our lives daily and with devotion of the pure, positive and pleasant fragrance of God's love, are we able to eradicate the wicked, willful wrong of our life.

The love of the disciple of Christ "does not rejoice at injustice and unrighteousness, but rejoices when right and truth prevail." In other words, a disciple is like the three monkeys with hands over the mouth, the ears and the eyes—they speak no evil, hear no evil and see no evil. Genuine love sees the bright side of things, spots the good, and senses a way to accept the constructive view of the situation. When we allow Christ to instill and increase this type of love in our lives, we will find "it will bear up under anything and everything that comes, is ever ready to believe the best of every person, its hopes are fadeless under all circumstances and it endures everything [without weakening" 1 Corinthians 13:7 AMP). This love will protect, preserve, provide hope and produce trust.

Friends, the love of God will never fail, never fade out, never forsake, and will ever favor us. That is God's promise in 1 Corinthians 13:8.

Horace Wood once said, "Before Christ, a man loves things and uses people. After Christ, he loves people and uses things." The Scriptures prove this out; however, have you found it to be realty in your life? Every sincere, surrendered and serving disciple will!

The love of God is not some factious made up myth. It is authentic and available to everyone. Any life filled with gloom and guilt can be freed with golden beams of hope and heaven found in the love of God. It will not only fill your life to the rim but overflow it into every relationship of life.

CHAPTER SIX

"He Is A Light!"

In the mid-nineteenth century, a person was employed by the town to light street lights. The person generally used a burning wick on a long pole. At dusk, they would light the candles, oil, or some similar consumable liquid or solid lighting source with wicks. At dawn, they would return and put them out using a bell or small hook on the same pole. The person would also perform the duty of renewing the candles, oil, or gas mantles. In some towns, the lamplighters served in a role of a town watchman, whose duties were to warn the inhabitants of any dangers.

Believers of Christ, who is the light of the world, must perform the task of "letting their lights shine before men" (Matthew 5:16 NIV).

Now, let us establish something first before we get into the task of shining. In the First Epistle of John, we find these words, "God is light: in him there is no darkness at all. If we claim to have fellowship with him . . . we walk in the light, as he is in the light" (1 John 1:5-7 KJV).

In the Apostle Paul's writings in Galatians, we are told that as disciples, we live this life in the flesh by "adherence to and reliance on and complete trust in the Son of God" (Galatians 2:20 AMP).

Therefore, once Christ has cleansed us from our sin and cleared the darkness of sin from our lives, we are able to be transparent enough to allow Christ, Who is the light of life, to shine through us unto others. In the Amplified Version of Mathew 5:16, we read, "Let your light so shine before men that they may see your moral excellence and your praiseworthy, noble and good deeds."

Putting it another way, the Apostle Paul said, "that ye may be blameless and harmless, the sons of God, without rebuke, in the midst of a crooked and perverse nation, among whom ye shine as lights in the world" (Philippians 2:15 KJV).

In writing to the church at Ephesus, the apostle stated, "For ye were sometimes darkness, but now are ye light in the Lord: walk as children of light" (Ephesians 5:8 KJV).

These preceding verses should comfort us and challenge us. They should comfort us in the fact that God has chosen to rescue us from the darkness of sin and fill our life with the glorious light of His presences. Then to know that we are privileged to be a beacon of happiness, honor and hope to a generation of people seeking, searching and scurrying about in the shadows for something real and reliable.

Now, note with me another thing that is found in the light section of the Sermon on the Mount. "Let your light so shine before men that they may see your moral excellence and your praiseworthy, noble and good deeds, and recognize and honor and praise and glorify your Father Who is in Heaven" (Matthew 5:16 AMP).

The purpose and plan of God residing within our life is to bless us and to beacon a ray of hope and help to those without Christ. In other words, we have been chosen to be a "lamplighter" of our generation.

We are to radiate the light of the healing, helpful and hopeful Word of God as we walk with God and work in life.

I read a story several years a go about the lighthouse at Calais, Maine. A traveler visiting the lighthouse said to the keeper, "what if one of the lights should go out at night?"

"Never! Impossible!" the keeper cried. "Yonder are ships sailing to all parts of the world. If tonight one of my burners were out, in six months I should hear form America and India, saying that on such a night the lights of Calais Lighthouse gave no warning and some vessel had been wrecked."

What a lesson to the disciples of our Lord! Our lights must shine steadily and always, that other storm-tossed souls may be guided to Christ!

God is not asking his followers to ring bells or fire guns to call attention to their light: He simply request that we just shine. As ambassadors, representatives, followers of Jesus Christ, we ought to be lighting fires of joy and focusing attention on the true emancipator of life—Jesus Christ.

In fact, each day we must rise with the declaration of "Good morning, Lord;" not "Good Lord, its morning." With each expressed "Good morning," let it be a statement of God offers us His Outstanding Devotion to Make us Obedient and Ready for a New day with Him, to Inspire others and Never forget God loves us!"

CHAPTER SEVEN

"He Is A Law-Keeper"

Laws are made to give control and provide secure and safe guidelines for living. The laws of God in regard to the Ten Commandments are valid and valuable to man today; as they were in the day God wrote them on tables of stone for Moses to give to the children of Israel. Jesus did not come to establish the church by doing away with the Ten Commandments but to fulfill them (Matthew 5:17) in enabling us to keep them through His amazing love and amazing grace.

In fact, the Word of God says, "for not the hearers of the law are just before God, but the doers of the law shall be . . . justified" (Romans 2:13 KJV). In fact, Christ came to put His laws into their mind, and write them in their hearts (Hebrews 8:10).

As the disciples of Jesus, called to listen, live, learn, lean on, love and light up the world; we must have a solid and sure resolution that will guide us, govern us and give us the power, pleasure and purpose for living. And we do—it is found in the law of God saturated with His love and seasoned with His grace. The Apostle Paul said, "God sending his own Son . . . that the righteousness of the law might be fulfilled in us, who walk not after the flesh, but after the Spirit" (Romans 8:3-4 KJV).

We can't keep the Ten Commandments nor live holy, honest and honorable lives without the soul steering help of Jesus who walked in the flesh even as we, yet without sin or breaking of the commandments.

It is important that we understand that the Ten Commandments were written for two reasons. First, they were written to convict man of His self-centered actions. As man considers the laws of God, He can evaluate His priorities and see where His personal devotions are (Romans 3:20; 7:7).

Consider this illustration: Go outside, roll in a mud puddle. Now walk back into the house and stand in front of a mirror. Ask the mirror to clean all the mud off of your body. Can it do that? No, of course not. All the mirror can do is show you that you have mud on you. Its only purpose is to let you know you need to be cleansed. The Law of God is no different, it reveals Secondly, they were written to give us gutter bumpers in walking the path of life. In case, you wonder what I mean by gutter bumpers; it is a long solid tube placed in the gutter of bowling lanes to keep the ball from leaving the lane and rolling down the gutter missing the pins.

As a disciple, we need the laws of God (Ten Commandments) to warn us and keep us from wandering away from the straight and narrow lanes of life that Jesus calls us to walk (Matthew 7:14). The laws of God are for our guidance and perfecting.

Solomon in all his wisdom concluded that the whole duty of man was to "reverence God and keep His commandments" (Ecclesiastes 12:13-14 KJV). Therefore, if we are to be a disciple of Jesus, we must be a law-keeper. We must see that it is more than nice (as our generation would like to label keeping the commandments), but necessary. Jesus said, "if thou wilt enter into life, keep the commandments" (Matthew 19:17 KJV).

Keeping the laws of God enable us to truly love God and love our neighbor as Jesus directed. For in the context of the commandments are directives of loving God (the first four commandments) and loving our neighbor (the last six commandments), Keeping the law of God is actually open evidence that you do love your neighbor and that you do love God wholeheartedly.

Consider this: Are you showing love for the Lord when you place praise and honor to something or someone else above God? Are you showing love for the true God when you worship or even work to obtain images, items or ideals that take more of your devotion of time, talent and treasure that you give to God? Are you showing love for the Lord when you use the Name of the Lord slanderously or without spiritual connotations? Are you really loving Him when you fail to remember the importance of the day designated for gathering together with the body of Christ (the church) and giving worship due His Name? See why it is so important that a disciple keep the law?

Think about it. You definitely do not show love toward others when you disobey and disrespect your parents. Your love for others is not demonstrated by hating or killing your fellow man; or by committing adultery against your spouse; or stealing from someone; or lying about your family, friends or even foes; or coveting anything that belongs to someone else. A disciple understands this and keeps the laws of God (The Ten Commandments).

Ralph Brewer made it plain when he said, "The Ten Commandments still cover all human relations and all spiritual relations."

I remember reading a short editorial once that stated, "When the editor of a small newspaper was short of material to fill his column one week, he asked his typesetter to fill in with the Ten Commandments. After that week's issue had been circulated, the editor received a letter from one reader saying, "Cancel my subscription. You are getting too personal." The laws of God are written with a personal touch and tone.

A disciple of Jesus will be a law keeper because He desires to please Christ, praise Him and present Him to a compromising, complacent and corrupt world. A disciple of Jesus will desire to go beyond the written letter of the law. God's love for His disciples will raise the standard. A disciple of Jesus will refrain from violating the law in action and in attitude. It should be the desire and devotion of the disciple to fulfill the words of Philippians 4:8, by keeping his focus on thoughts that are true, honest, just, pure, lovely and of good report.

I feel it is important that we remember one more important thing regarding being a law keeper. If the law is broken and we experience the tender mercy of God in forgiving us; we must not take liberty in continuing to break the law of God (Romans 6).

Consider this illustration: Picture being pulled over by a cop for speeding. You are not "under" the law until you speed. You broke the law and now the "curse" of the law is your just desert, which in this case is the ticket. However, if you ask the patrolman for mercy, and he gives it . . . are you allowed to speed now? No, of course not! You don't pull away spraying gravel on the cop because you don't want to insult his mercy.

As a disciple of Jesus, let us remember to be grateful for the glorious mercy and grace that sets us free from the bondage of the law. The law exists with purpose yet God's love easies and erases the penalty and the power of the law in order for man to be willing and able to keep the law.

In fact let me conclude this chapter with a humorous, yet to the point story. A high school senior was trying out for a summer job on the small town newspaper. "Would you be any good at rewrite?" The editor asked him.

"Sure, "said the teen-ager brashly.

"Okay, let's see you rewrite this and make it short and to the point." With that, the editor handed the boy a copy of the Ten Commandments.

The boy looked at them, scratched his head, and then in a burst of inspiration scribbled something across the top of the paper, which he then handed back.

The editor took one look and said, "You're hired, boy!"

The teen-ager had written the word "Don't!"

Folks, the laws of God (The Ten Commandments) are written that we would follow Jesus in a positive, pure way and that occurs if we will abide in His love and fulfill the commandments by not breaking them.

A genuine disciple of Christ will be a law keeper.

CHAPTER EIGHT

"He Is A Load Bearer"

Bearing one another's burdens is not limited to carry the burden of sin, suffering, sickness or some self-weakness. There are many kinds of burdens we have to bear personally, in public and in private situations. The key to compassion is understanding just how heavy other people's burdens are.

An American professor told about visiting Albert Schweitzer in Africa when Dr. Schweitzer was 85 years old. In his younger days Schweitzer had been a great organist and musicologist, and theologian, and then decided to go to medical school to serve Christ among the most needy in Africa. Now Schweitzer was 85, and one day he was walking up a hill with the American visitor when he suddenly strode across the hill to where an African woman was struggling with a huge armload of wood for her cook fire. He took the whole load of wood and carried it up the hill. When they all got to the top of the hill, the American asked Schweitzer why he did things like that, given the heat conditions of the environment and his age. Albert Schweitzer looked at him and pointed at the woman and said simply, "No one should ever have to carry a burden like that alone."

In our modern community and man-made churches, we are guilty of standing idle when it comes to other people's lives. Our culture's value of "live and let live" invades the church and establishes a radical individualism that cuts off real comradeship and care for one another. We are unaware of the burdens others bear. We either do not see or we are not interested enough to perceive. We do not hear, or we have not been truly listening. Even in prayer request times, we are aware that suffering is reported but not acknowledged or assigned to aid in the situation. To be aware of someone drowning will not aid the person. You must jump into the water.

The Apostle Paul declares, "Bear one another's burdens" (Galatians 6:2). When we become law keepers, we will become load bearers. For it is the same love that erects a reminder of the law and enables one to keep the law; that will enlighten one to be aware of burdens and become available to assist in bearing those burdens.

Yet, we live in a society where statements like, "He made his bed, let him lie in it." Or maybe you have heard, "They deserve it." "He just can't handle the pressure." "I saw it coming." "Maybe they'll listen to me next time." "I don't want to get involved." "I'm just glad it is them and not me." All of these statements are uttered to build up self and an attempt to excuse one from helping carry one another's burdens.

The preceding statements may be the modern American way but it is not God's way. It is not characteristic of a true disciple of Christ. We are to bear one another's burdens.

Take note of this little story. A mouse looked through the crack in the wall to see the farmer and his wife open a package. "What food might this contain?" the mouse wondered—he was devastated to discover it was a mousetrap.

Retreating to the farmyard, the mouse proclaimed the warning: "There is a mousetrap in the house! There is a mousetrap in the house!"

The chicken clucked and scratched, raised her head and said, "Mr. Mouse, I can tell this is a grave concern to you, but it is of no consequence to me. I cannot be bothered by it."

The mouse turned to the pig and told him, "There is a mousetrap in the house! There is a mousetrap in the house!"

The pig sympathized, but said, "I am so very sorry, Mr. Mouse, but there is nothing I can do about it but pray. Be assured you are in my prayers."

The mouse turned to the cow and said, "There is a mousetrap in the house! There is a mousetrap in the house!"

The cow said, "Wow, Mr. Mouse, I'm sorry for you, but it's no skin off my nose."

So, the mouse returned to the house, head down and dejected, to face the farmer's mousetrap . . . alone.

That very night a sound was heard throughout the house—like the sound of a mousetrap catching its prey. The farmer's wife rushed to see what was caught. In the darkness, she did not see it was a venomous snake whose tail the trap had caught. The snake bit the farmer's wife.

The farmer rushed her to the hospital, and she returned home with a fever. Everyone knows you treat a fever with fresh chicken soup, so the farmer took his hatchet to the farmyard for the soup's main ingredient.

But his wife's sickness continued, so friends and neighbors came to sit with her around the clock. To feed them, the farmer butchered the pig.

The farmer's wife did not get well; she died. So many people came for her funeral, the farmer had the cow slaughtered to provide enough meat for all of them.

The mouse looked upon it all from his crack in the wall with great sadness. So, the next time you hear someone is facing a problem and think it doesn't concern you, remember—when one of us is threatened, we are all at risk. We are all involved in this journey called life. We must keep an eye out for one another and make an extra effort to encourage one another.

We pass people every day on the streets and in the stores; yet we don't know what loads they may be carrying. We talk with one another at work, school and in church; yet we somehow never see the "arm load of firewood" they struggle to carry. Yet, their human spirits are hunched over from carrying heavy loads that are invisible to others. There are loads of grief from past and present losses. Some may be weighed down by financial worries, by fear of unemployment or failing businesses or failure in receiving child support; but they are not going to announce it. Some are facing serious illness or separation from sons and daughters who have rebelled.

However, let us as disciples allow God to give us a discerning spirit (not of the specific problem, but of the hurt); and encourage us to pray for the individual, to prepare our hearts to speak encouragement to them and present our self to Him for direction in assisting them.

While it is true, every person has their own troubles and trials; yet how wonderful it is to know that God cares for us and there are others who care and are willing to aid us in carrying our backpack of burdens. Therefore, we must aid others in coping with their burdens and accept the help from others in coping with our burdens.

People are not perfect and they will fail. Therefore, some of the burdens are moral and spiritual. People make bad choices. However, the spiritual strong must be willing to forgive, forget and fortify the spiritual weak, the wayward and even those who have wronged us. The Apostle Paul gives encouraging words in Galatians chapter six. Read this chapter for yourself.

As born again believers growing into disciples, we must "stand firm in the liberty wherein Christ has made us free" (Galatians 5:1). As a disciple of Christ, we must stand firm in His holiness, His righteousness and His love. We are identified as His disciples when we walk in His freedom.

Christ holds us accountable to care for ourselves and to be responsible for others, particularly in the body of the church (Galatians 6). We are supposed to be walking the same path with the same purpose. Therefore, if we are to march properly and make progress, we must keep one another strong and stable by carrying one another's burdens. This is an identifying characteristic of the disciple of Christ.

When General William Booth, the founder of the Salvation Army, was an old man, he was invited to address a large convention of Army workers and volunteers. When it was determined he was unable to attend, he was asked to send a greeting instead. His reply was a one word greeting: "Others."

The Apostle Paul had echoed the same message when he penned his letter to the church at Philippi. He said, "Do nothing from selfishness or empty conceit, but with humility of mind let each of you regard one another as more important than himself; do not merely look out for your own personal interests, but also for the interests of others" (Philippians 2:3-4).

Let us never get so wrapped up in ourselves that we don't know what others need. If we do we will never be able to assist others. It is only when we have a right view of our self, under the umbrella of grace that we can help carry the burdens of others.

Being a disciple of Christ is being available to assist others in carrying their burdens.

CHAPTER NINE

"He Is A Living Example"

I once read "No man's actions stop with himself." Our actions and attitudes affect and influence others. As a disciple of Christ, we are to influence others in a positive way—pointing them to Christ and personally lifting them up. The Apostle Paul, while traveling with Silas and Timothy, wrote to the believers in Thessalonica encouraging and explaining the role of caring for others and becoming role models of Christianity to the community and the church (1 Thessalonians 2).

In this writing, the Apostle challenged believers to "walk worthy of God"—His calling and cleansing. He stated that we are to become "imitators of Christ." In other words, we are representatives of Christ and it is our task to reveal Him to others.

The depths of our concern for others determine the length and breadth of our influence upon others. Do we bear fruit to set examples of caring for the material; as well, as the moral conditions of man? "For I was hungry and you gave me food; I was thirsty and you gave me drink; I was a stranger and you took me in; I was naked and you clothed me; I was sick and you visited me; I was In prison and you came toe me" (Matthew 25:35-36 KJV).

It is so important to encourage others by example and exhortation. For once a man has been with Christ, experienced the contentment of His grace, the comfort of His love, the cleansing of His forgiveness, and the constant indwelling of His Spirit; he inevitably comes to a point when he can no longer be satisfied unless he is serving the Lord. The Word of God states, "It is enough for a disciple that he be like his teacher, and a servant like his master" (Matthew 10:25 KJV). To be like Jesus should be the goal of every follower of Jesus.

God enriches and enables man to give his life to a cause, attempt to cause change and to do something concrete with his life. Therefore, it is important what we say, where we go, what we wear, and what we do. It matters how we act and react in the crises, confrontations and circumstances of everyday life. It makes a difference regarding who we associate with and to what degree of commitment we have toward our work, our worship and our world.

Because of this fact, let us not strive to make our self holy by working, but by believing and by living entirely on the strength of Christ who is our life (Philippians 4:13). We must remember that being a living example is more than a testimony of Biblical knowledge; it is a transfer of spiritual revelation that causes a spiritual conversion and commitment (1 Corinthians 8:1-2).

A disciple is a true transparent temple of Christ. He imitates Christ by following His principles, His purpose, His purity, His perfect love, His patience, His perseverance, His persecutions and His practices in conduct and conversation (2 Timothy 3:10-11). A disciple is a living example in deeds and doctrine (Titus 2:7-8). His goal is to further mature himself in Christ, function in a way that produces a clear revelation of Jesus Christ and produce fresh fruit (of the Spirit) that will cause others to desire the quality of character (fruit of the Spirit) that he demonstrates.

Therefore, we need to take the counsel of Susannah Wesley, mother of John and Charles Wesley. She told her sons to remember this rule: "whatever weakens your reason, impairs the tenderness of your conscience, obscures your sense of God or takes off the relish of spiritual things is sin" and will sap your authority to walk with Christ and witness to others regarding Christ.

Let us remember the words of George Eliot: "May every soul that touches mine, be it the slightest contact, get there from some good . . . some little grace . . . one kindly thought, one aspiration yet unfelt, one bit of courage form the darkening sky; one gleam of faith to brave the thickening ills of life; one glimpse of brighter skies beyond the gathering mists to make this life worth while."

Is this our desire and delight as disciples of Jesus? Are we bearing the fruit of the Holy Spirit (Galatians 5:22-23)? For it is His words that help form our words. It is His power that enriches our personality. It is His love that enables our lifestyles to radiate His life to others. For Jesus said, "I am the vine, you are the branches. He who abides in Me, and I in him, bears much fruit; for without Me you can do nothing" (John 15:5).

While it is true that we have flaws and at times feel we are a failure in accomplishing anything good for the kingdom of God. It may even appear we are wasting our abilities and attempts at doing the work of God or walking the way of God. Yet be assured that Christ knows our motive and our desire to be meaningful. Keep in mind, as born again believers, we have experienced a new birth and should enjoy the change Jesus brought about in our life. Walk the path of godliness, goodness and grace and let God judge the accomplishments. It will make a difference now and in eternity.

Let me conclude this chapter with a little story. An elderly Chinese woman had two large pots, each hung on the ends of a pole which she carried across her neck. One of the pots had a crack in it while the other pot was perfect and always delivered a full portion of water.

At the end of the long walks from the stream to the house, the cracked pot arrived only half full.

For a full two years this went on daily, with the woman bringing home only one and a half pots of water. Of course, the perfect pot was proud of its accomplishments. But the poor cracked pot was ashamed of its own imperfections, and miserable that it could only do half of what it had been made to do.

After two years of what it perceived to be bitter failure, it spoke to the woman one day by the stream "I am ashamed of myself, because this crack in my side causes water to leak out all the way back to your house."

The old woman smiled, "Did you notice that there are flowers on your side of the path, but not on the other pot's side?"

That's because I have always known about your flaw, so I planted flower seeds on your side of the path, and every day while we walk back, you water them. For two years I have been able to pick these beautiful flowers to decorate the table. Without you being just the way you are, there would not be this beauty to grace the house."

Each of us has our own unique flaw. But it's the cracks and flaws we each have that make our lives so very interesting and rewarding. Thank God and trust Him to use you just as you. Be a living example in your walk of life knowing God can produce something beautiful and something beneficial for you and others.

CHAPTER TEN

"He Is Laughter!"

I enjoy sharing jokes and reacting jubilant at sporting events. I enjoy watching reaction of children and even adults in certain circumstances. I even get a kick out of watching "America's Funniest Home Videos." However, there is no way to describe the feeling of knowing the joy of the Lord or watching a person being filled with the joy of salvation. I am convinced that Christ gives every believer a divine joy. "These things have I spoken unto you, that my joy might remain in you, and that your joy might be full" (John 15:11 KJV).

Now I will have to admit that many church-minded individuals act and appear as if they have been sucking on a lemon. They have not learned nor live in His joy. We must be willing to let the joy erupt into a visible and valid expression. We should allow the divine given joy to erupt into laughter. It is His will that we enjoy our experience with Him in this life and get ready for a hallelujah time in the life to come.

Now, I do not believe that we will ever find a true joy in the natural things of this life. There may be many so-called stimuli that create artificial laughter And there maybe many silly and funny things declared and done that produce a laugh; however, true joy comes only from the Lord.

The joy of the Lord is a spring flowing from the well of salvation that Jesus plants within our lives. It quenches our thirst for the natural satisfactions of life and gives us a quest for the divine blessings found in walking with our Lord.

In that walk of life, we experience trials and troubles. However, God's Word declares that His followers will be enriched with the ability to laugh. "Blessed are you who weep now, for you will laugh" (Luke 6:21 NIV).

There is a small, simple and superb chorus that echoes words of reality. "I've never see the rainbow, till after the rain; and I've never felt His healing power till after the pain. I've never seen the sun shine till after the night; and I've never known the victory till after the fight." God has always provided us with joy in the morning following a difficult night. The Psalmist declared, ".Weeping may endure for a night, but joy cometh in the morning" (Psalm 30:5 KJV).

Humor originated with God. Just look around you at the odd creations that exist, including yourself. You have to chuckle at cute little things children say while learning and the odd shapes and shades that make up our world.

Gerald Kennedy once said, "Science cannot restore the joy of life and help us laugh again. Joy and laughter are products of faith. Men can laugh only when they believe."

Therefore, I define joy as a deep-seated contentment and commitment within the heart of man that erupts with an emotion of delight. It is an intense happiness within a life.

As a follower of Christ and one who has His Spirit within our life, we have His joy. And if we possess His presences deep-seated in our spirit, not being dependent on external circumstances or conditions; there should be expressed evidence to back it up.

For instance, gloom and despair should not dominate our lives as disciples of Christ. We should be able to possess contentment and have a commitment regardless of what may come against us. It is true that the enemy, Satan and sin, attempts to derail us and defeat us by robbing us of the joy and the justification we have in Christ.

In Solomon's Proverbs, it states, "A merry heart does good like a medicine; but a broken spirit dries the bones" (Proverbs 17:22 NIV). When distress, disease, disappointments and delusion attempts to disconnect us from the flow of the anointing of God's love and dry up the stream of His joy, we must stand and laugh in the enemy's face and let the light of the glory of God dispel the dreaded darkness.

"Light is shed upon the righteous, and joy on the upright in heart" (Psalm 97:11 NIV). When there is grace in the heart, there is joy. It has been said, "though a Christian lacks the sun, he has a day-star in his heart."

Consider the words of the prophet Isaiah, "to bestow on them a crown of beauty instead of ashes, the oil of gladness instead of mourning, and a garment of praise, instead of a spirit of despair" (Isaiah 61:3 NIV). Today, in the midst of yokes of bondage, Christ desires to enrich us and enable us to be disciples filled with "a joy that is unspeakable and full of glory" (1 Peter 1:8).

The very nature of the spirit of God, that wishes to make every believer a joyful disciple, is to destroy every yoke of bondage and give you a defense against those things that will come against you.

Did you know that it is a proven medical fact that negative emotions (unhappiness, lack of joy) releases harmful chemicals in your body that can cause disease and depression? It is also proven that positive emotions and laughter release beneficial chemicals in your body and brai that promote health and healing. Joy and laughter is good for your physical and psychological health; as well, as your spiritual health.

Don't let Satan short circuit your spiritual joy and rob you of your delight in life? You need the joy of the Lord. It is your strength. Do what it takes to get it and do what it takes to keep it. The Christian joy and laughter is essential for a beneficial life. And it comes only from a real relationship with Christ and a rich knowledge of God's Word.

Spiritual joy is built on the amazing love of God, on the abiding promises of Scriptures and on the atoning blood of Christ. It is a joy that is not dependent on outward things. The prophet Habakkuk declared, "Even though the fig trees have no blossoms, and there are no grapes on the vine; even though the olive crops fail, and the cattle barns lie empty and barren; even though the flocks die in the fields, and the cattle barns are empty, yet I will rejoice in the Lord! I will be joyful in the God of my salvation" (Habakkuk 3:17-18 NIV).

Every believer should have a firm hope that Jesus is coming again to receive us unto Himself. With this hope we are able to rejoice. "I will see you again, and your heart shall rejoice, and your joy no man taketh from you" (John 16:22 KJV).

Martin Luther once stated, "If you're not allowed to laugh in heaven, I don't want to go there."

I believe there is plenty of joy in heaven now and in the days to come. Jesus stated in Luke's account of the Gospel that "rejoicing in heaven over one sinner who repents" (Luke 15:7 NIV). Jesus stated in Matthew's account of the Gospel, "Well done, thou good and faithful servant . . . enter thou into the joy of the Lord" (Matthew 25:21).

God doesn't just want humanity to experience a fresh start in his relationship with Him; but He wants man to enjoy a dose of refreshment every step of the way.

Wilford A. Peterson said, "Laughter is the best medicine for a long and happy life. He who laughs—lasts."

Let me close this chapter with another quote. This one is from Grenville Kleiser. He uses the word "humor" instead of joy or laughter, but the message is clear. Here is what he said:

"Good humor is a tonic for the mind and body,

It is the best antidote for anxiety and depression. It is a business asset. It attracts and keeps friends. It lightens human burdens. It is the direct route to serenity and contentment."

If you are a believer and desire to be a fulfilling disciple of Christ, you must have a sense of humor and enjoy life.

CHAPTER ELEVEN

"He Is Longsuffering"

It is a known fact that the world is a giant landscape of countries, cultures, climates and conditions that require individuals to exercise a virtue called patience. However, few manage to develop such a trait. Short-temperedness, sometimes called impatience, is a common trait of many individuals within our world. It is the opposite of longsuffering, a virtue Jesus demonstrated throughout His ministry and a virtue deemed important for his followers.

"Longsuffering" is one of the fruits the Holy Spirit desires to develop in our lives as we live by His divine directions received through the written pages of God's Holy Word.

In defining "longsuffering," you may consider the meaning of other terms, such as, 'forbearance," "patience," and "self-restraint."

Longsuffering has been defined as "that quality of self-restraint in the face of provocation which does not hastily retaliate or promptly punish. It is the opposite of anger, and is associated with mercy."

It is a quality of character that tends to remain calm, cool and collective; unwilling to surrender to circumstances or succumb under pressure. Another definition states, "the ability to willingly accept or tolerate delay or hardship."

Today's human being is unwilling to put up with what doesn't conform, ditching the spouse if things aren't working out just right, deciding on short-term investments to make quick bucks, dumping chemicals in a nearby stream to just get rid of the stuff quickly, distracted by the commercials and unwilling to wait to get something watchable on television disgusted at the driver when the car in front of you doesn't move as soon as the light changes. Such individuals declare they can't afford to be patient; yet in all reality, we can't afford not to learn and live longsuffering.

The Apostle Paul stated that it was an exercise that needed to be directed toward one another. In his writings we see the message echoed, "With all lowliness and meekness, with longsuffering, forbearing one another in love" (Ephesians 4:2 KJV). On another occasion, he penned "Put on therefore, as the elect of God, holy and beloved, bowels of mercies, kindness, humbleness of mind, meekness, longsuffering" (Colossians 3;12 KJV).

We would all agree that the world would be a better and more balanced place to live if the inhabitants would learn to control their tempers. An exercise of longsuffering in the schools would provide a peaceful arena and atmosphere for learning. A demonstration of patience in the home would bring greater harmony and a happier environment of life. In fact, living would be easier if men showed as much patience at home as they do when they're waiting for a fish to bite. A display of patience in the streets would reduce stress and promote safety. A decline of short-temperedness in the neighborhood would enhance acceptance and association. It has been said that anger is a condition in which the tongue works faster than the mind.

If mercy and mildness, demonstrated in longsuffering, is ever to spread across the nation and around the world, it must be taught and caught in the pews of our churches. Individuals who have been born again by faith in Christ must develop this discipline that produces true disciples. The Apostle Paul relays to Timothy some wise advise, "Howbeit for this cause I obtained mercy, that in me first Jesus Christ might show forth all longsuffering, for a pattern to them which should hereafter believe on him to life everlasting" (1 Timothy 1:16 KJV).

While it is true, every local church is made up of an assortment of personalities and each congregation is a "mixed bag" of people from various backgrounds and cultures; the church must become a breeding ground of such virtue. The church has members who are on different rungs of the maturity ladder, both socially and spiritually; yet a pulling together rather than a pulling apart will provide understanding and unity. Therefore, longsuffering is necessary to be able to get along and "grow in the knowledge and grace of the Lord."

A spirit of longsuffering is a result of having the teaching of the Holy Spirit in one's heart. A life dedicated to the Spirit and dictated by the Spirit, absorbs His qualities and alters our relationships with others.

God's attitude and action toward man is the grand demonstration of longsuffering. He has put up with man's ignorance, idolatry, immorality, insincerity, iniquity, and impatience. In doing so, He has proven His faithfulness and willingness to forgive. Thank God for that! Now, we must remember that His longsuffering has its limits in regard to our sinfulness and stubbornness. The Disciple Peter declared that God's promise is two-fold. He is "not willing that any should perish, but that all should come to repentance;" and a Day of Judgment will take place concerning those who have rejected Him (2 Peter 3).

In living our everyday life one earth, possessing patience would prevent harsh judgments of actions that spring from immaturity or a lack of knowledge. We must overcome reacting hastily and harshly. We must not keep a short fuse on what we say or the things we do. We must possess and practice longsuffering. "For ye have need of patience, that, after ye have done the will of God, ye might receive the promise" (Hebrews 10:36 KJV).

You know, God sometimes permits us to be perplexed so that we may learn patience and better recognize our dependence upon Him.

John Newton put it this way, "Be patient enough to live one day at a time as Jesus taught us, letting yesterday go, and leaving tomorrow till it arrives."

Yet man cries out, "God give me patience—RIGHT NOW!" However, when some situation tries our patience, we should have a laugh over it, and it will seem less burdensome.

The Apostle Paul was an object of longsuffering, and made it an integral part of his own life. He stated to Timothy, "But thou hast fully known my doctrine, manner of life, purpose, faith, longsuffering, charity, patience" (2 Timothy 3:10 KJV). In Paul we see an individual who endured pressures, problems, persecutions and perplexities beyond anything that we will ever endure. The reason lies in his lifestyle of being patience for God to work out the plan for his life. He did not always understand, but he never gave up or gave in.

Listen to his words, "For which cause we faint not; but though out outward man perish, yet the inward man is renewed day by day. For out light affliction, which is but for a moment, worketh for us a far more exceeding and eternal weight of glory; While we look not at the things which are see, but at the things which are not seen: for the things which are seen are temporal; but the things which are not seen are eternal" (2 Corinthians 4:16-18 KJV).

Longsuffering is one of the virtues that makes the Christian "neither to be barren nor unfruitful in the knowledge of our Lord Jesus Christ" (2 Peter 1:5).

James P. Needham, shared in an article, six suggestions that will help answer the question, "How does one acquire longsuffering?

1) "One must be persistent in a desire to develop patience. It does not come by accident."

2) "Exercise longsuffering toward oneself. He states that we are impatient with our own shortcomings and mistakes. We seem to get angry toward ourselves when things go wrong. We become frustrated at our own absentmindedness." I heard a cute story that might help us relate to this area of our life. A preacher asked a lady if she ever thought about the hereafter. Her reply was, "Yes, every day when I go into a room, or open my refrigerator, or go to the grocery store, I say to my self, 'what am I here after?" We must learn to stay cool, calm and collective; and not be too judgmental with ourself

3) "The development of longsuffering is strictly the responsibility of the individual. Every man is the sole proprietor of his own physical mind and body." The Apostle Paul said, "But I keep under my body, and bring it into subjection" (1 Corinthians 9:27).

4) "Following the "golden rule" is conducive to the development of longsuffering." "Therefore all things whatsoever ye would that men should do to you, do ye even so to them" (Matthew 7:12).

5) "Study God's Word diligently." Let the Word be an inspiration to you and learn to observe the quality of character demonstrated by Christ and exemplified by true followers of Him.

6) "Consider the uselessness and possible harm that can be done by impatience. The things we say and do out of a lack of longsuffering are seldom good or a source of personal satisfaction. In fact we often need to apologize for the things we say and do out of impatience.

It has been said that patience is the ability to keep your motor idling when you feel like stripping the gears. We can not afford to damage our life if we wish to be in good working order for service in the kingdom of God. We must avoid anything that would hamper, hinder or hurt our devotion to Christ and our daily effort to shine, share and salt the world for Jesus.

Let us prove our devotion and discipline our lives to be a growing, glowing disciple of the Lord Jesus Christ.

And speaking of glowing let me include this little story about silences paying dividends.

A member of a certain church, who previously had been attending services regularly, stopped going. After a few weeks, the preacher decided to visit him.

It was a chilly evening. The preacher found the man at home alone, sitting before a blazing fire. Guessing the reason for his preacher's visit, the man welcomed him, led him to a comfortable chair near the fireplace and waited.

The preacher made himself at home but said nothing. In the grave silence, he contemplated the dance of the flames around the burning logs. After some minutes, the preacher took the fire tongs, carefully picked up a brightly burning ember and placed it to one side of the hearth all alone then he sat back in his chair, still silent.

The host watched all this in quiet contemplation. As the one lone ember's flame flickered and diminished, there was a momentary glow and then its fire was no more . . . soon it was cold and dead.

Not a word had been spoke since the initial greeting. The preacher glanced at his watch and realized it was time to leave. He slowly stood up, picked up the cold, dead ember and laced it back in the middle of the fire. Immediately it began to glow, once more with the light and warmth of the burning coals around it.

As the preacher reached the door to leave, his host said with a tear running down his cheek, "Thank you so much for your visit and especially for the fiery sermon. I shall be back in church next Sunday."

We live in a world today, which tries to say too much with too little. Consequently, few listen. Sometimes the best sermons are the ones left unspoken.

CHAPTER TWELVE

"He is Lowly"

I heard a story once about a city boy visiting on a farm for the first time. He saw a field of ripening wheat. He noticed that some of the yellowing stems stood up tall and straight while others gracefully bent their heads. To the farm lad who was showing him around, he said, "those stalks that stand up so tall and straight must be the best." "They look as if they were proud of what they were doing."

The country lad laughed. "That's because you don't know much about wheat," he explained. He plucked a head of each and rubbing them in his hands showed that the tall, straight stalks held very little grain, while the bending heads were filled with the promise of a rich harvest.

Folks, one of the surest evidences of greatness is a humble spirit. The Bible declares, "The Lord is nigh unto them that are of a broken heart; and saveth such as be of a contrite spirit" (Psalm 34:18 KJV).

Andrew Murray wrote probably the best book ever written on humility. It is titled, "Humility." One critic of the book stated, "Murray shows how humility is a mindset and lifestyle, not a feeling. He states that humility is a one-word definition of every Christian's life—or it should be."

Humility is not brokenness caused by sin, but a quality resulting from the grace of God working within the believer.

Man may achieve popularity, possessions, power and position. He may develop a dynamic personality or obtain degrees in education. Yet, he is not considered a true winner until he empties himself and allows God to fill him with His holy presences. "Be clothed with humility; for God resisteth the proud and giveth grace to the humble" (1 Peter 5:5 KJV).

Man has limitations. His natural ability is limited. His time on earth is limited. His resources are limited. However, when he humbles himself before an omnipotent, omnipresent, and all providing God; he is lifted into a sphere of accomplishing exactly what is expected of him. Therefore, our dependency on Christ makes a way for all things to come to pass. Just as the Scriptures declare, "He humbled Himself, and became obedient unto death" (Philippians 2:8 KJV). His humility gave His death its value and its victory.

Humility is not a door mat in your life for others to walk on, but a character for others to behold and build from. It is in our humility that springs strength, smiles and success. "Humble yourselves therefore under the mighty hand of God, that He may exalt you in due time" (1 Peter 5:6). When others behold such traits in our life, they delight and desire to know the secret.

Meekness, lowliness, humility are interchanging terms of being submissive and surrendered to the will of God. It is a distinguishing feature of the disciple. It is derived and developed from daily prayer, divine pursuit and daily practice. As one seeks to be a true humble servant of God, he will search and study the Word of God.

Blaise Pascal, a mathematician and philosopher, said, "humility is avoiding behavior such as boasting, bragging and valuing your opinion above others." We need to develop an attitude that regardless of the position one may possess in society, the profession one may engage in, the person's age or personal economic status; they are creator of God in need of His love and our love. In fact, the Apostle Paul said, "Clothe yourself, all of you, with humility toward one another" (1 Peter 5:5 KJV). He called upon the Philippians to "do nothing from selfishness or conceit, but in humility count others better than yourselves" (Philippians 2:3)

We need to be careful about being obsessed with our own appearance, our own opinions and our own possessions. Such extreme devotions to self will create roadblocks to humility. We must be careful not to let the arch enemy of humility—pride—creep into our life. We must watch out for insecurity because it is noted that insecure people lack confidence because they spend too much time examining themselves.

As we begin doing acts of humility, we soon allow it to become a habit. This is good, for it develops a positive life change and makes an impact on the quality of our life and those around us.

Every individual is challenged by God's Word to "live a life worthy of the calling to which you have been called, with all humility and meekness, with patience" (Ephesians 4:1-2). In doing so, we engage and enjoy a relationship with God and with God's creation, man. Humility is the scriptural and sure way to friendship with one another. It enables us to be open to one another, accepting each other just as we are.

One who is humble will never find any task too small, too insignificant, or too hard to do for someone. Just as Christ performed every task for others with dignity and devotion, so should we as His disciples.

A lowly heart provides a lifting spirit. A humble person can neither be put down nor exalted; he can neither be humiliated nor honored; he remains the same person under all circumstances.

One of the most beautiful stories that I have ever read was one that occurred at the beginning of his sermon. The pastor was about to announce his scripture text when Bill walked into the building. He had wild hair, worn a T-shirt with holes in it, jeans and no shoes. Bill looks around for a seat. The church is completely packed and he can't find a seat.

By now, people are really looking a bit uncomfortable, but no one says anything. Bill gets closer and closer and closer to the pulpit, and when he realizes there are no seats, he just squats down right on the carpet between the front pew and the platform.

By now, the people are really uptight, and the tension in the air is thick. About this time, the minister realizes that from way at the back of the church, a deacon is slowly making his way toward Bill.

Now the deacon is in his eighties, has silver-gray hair, and a three-piece suit. He is a godly man, very elegant, very dignified, very courtly. He walks with a cane and, as he starts walking toward this boy, everyone is saying to themselves that you can't blame him for what he's going to do. How can you expect a man of his age and of his background to understand some college kid on the floor?

It takes a lot time for the man to reach the boy.

The church is utterly silent except for the clicking of the man's cane. All eyes are focused on him. You can't even hear anyone breathing. The minster can't even preach the sermon until the deacon does what he has to do.

And now they see this elderly man drop his cane on the floor. With great difficulty, he lowers himself and sits down next to Bill and worships with him so he won't be alone.

Everyone chokes up with emotion.

When the minister gains control, he says, "What I'm about to preach, you will never remember. What you have just seen, you will never forget."

A simple act of humility will enrich our life, encourage another life and enlighten yet another.

CHAPTER THIRTEEN

"He Is At Liberty"

There is a word we hear constantly in these turbulent times, and that word is, freedom. It seems that everyone is in pursuit of it. Individuals look for freedom from debt. People search for freedom from the anxiety of not knowing what tomorrow may bring. Masses long to be out from under the rule of tyrants and enjoy political freedom. Many addicts long to know freedom from their habits.

Freedom is available. Through Jesus Christ a person can experience a liberty from being afraid; a liberty from the bonds of addictions; a liberty from the anxiety of daily living; a liberty from physical and emotional afflictions; a liberty from adversity; a liberty from the agony of making ends meet; and a liberty from the guilt of sin.

The Word of God challenges us to realize, receive and remain in the liberty of Christ. "In this liberty Christ has made us free—completely liberated us, stand fast then, and do not be hampered and held ensnared and submit again to a yoke of slavery—which you have once put off" (Galatians 5:1 AMP).

"In this liberty" speaks of a born again experience of the supernatural working of God. It is in Him and through Him that mere mortal man is set free to enjoy the liberty of life: Freedom without baggage—no stress, no sadness, no side-effects and no senseless guilt.

Jesus has paid the price for our freedom. The way has been paved. It remains only for us to acknowledge the truth and to humble ourselves to receive the gift of "liberty."

God's liberty is not found in a prescription or a program. It cannot be obtained on a payment plan or the purchase of a system. It is not based on political principles or popular vote. It is founded on the supreme sacrifice of Jesus Christ on the cross and our belief in Him. "You shall know the truth, and the truth shall make you free . . . And if the Son therefore shall make you free, ye shall be free indeed" (John 8:32, 36 KJV).

It is hard to believe that liberty is so freely offered, but so constantly refused by men. People look to political leaders, philosophers, physicians and programs to provide the answers. Yet, failure and false hope is the results.

Try Jesus! His way has worked, is working and will continue to be successful. Listen to the words of Jesus, "Come to Me, all you who labor, and are heavy-laden and over burdened, and I will cause you to rest—I will ease and relieve and refresh your souls. Take My yoke upon you, and learn of Me; for I am gentle (meek) and humble (lowly) in heart, and you will find rest—relief, ease and refreshment and recreation and blessed quiet—for your souls. For My yoke is wholesome (useful, good)—not harsh, hard, sharp or pressing, but comfortable, gracious and pleasant; and My burden is light and easy to be borne" (Matthew 11:28-30 AMP).

Dwight Moody once told of a man who said he would like to come to Jesus, but he was chained and could not break away. A Christian said to him, "But, man, why don't you come, chain and all?" He said, "I never thought of that. And I will." He did and Christ broke every fetter and allowed him to experience true liberty.

Think about it for a moment. Who of the following was really free? Noah, shut up by God in the dark, damp, drenched storm-tossed ark, or those on the outside living it up until they drown? Daniel in the den of lions, or King Darius pacing his palace floor? Joseph, sold into slavery, or his brothers counting the money? Paul, the prisoner, whom men thought was bound or Felix, the governor, who was thought to be free?

The outward circumstances (situation beyond our control) are irrelevant. True freedom is a spiritual condition, not a physical or emotional one. Freedom is fellowship with God. It is not dependant upon externals. It is not affected by circumstances. It has its being in the sphere of the mind and heart. "Thou wilt keep him in perfect peace, whose mind is stayed on thee" is the promise of God to man (Isaiah 26:3 KJV). When the presences of God abide within our lives, we know peace and possess liberty. Every external encounter and experience will take it course according to the plan of God. "Where the Spirit of the Lord is, there is liberty" (2 Corinthians 3:17 KJV). "We are assured and know that God being a partner in their labor, all things work together and are fitting into a plan for good to those who love God and are called to His design and purpose" (Romans 8:28 AMP).

"Then said Jesus to those Jews which believed on him, If ye continue in my word, then are ye my disciples indeed; and ye shall know the truth, and the truth shall make you free" (John 8:31-32 KJV).

Satisfying liberty comes about when we acknowledge that we do not enjoy this life and we really do not experience daily freedom; then turn to Jesus to transform our life. In our transformed life we are filled with His love, founded on His Word and functioning in His liberty.

Our life is blessed. "But he who looks carefully into the faultless law, the law of liberty, and is faithful to it and perseveres in looking into it, being not a heedless listener who forgets, but an active doer who obeys, he shall be blessed in his doing—in his life of obedience" (James 1:25 AMP).

We must never forget what William Penn said, "Liberty without obedience is confusion." There is no freedom unless we yield to God; receiving Him and resisting those things that rob us of our spiritual liberty. Frustration and failure will result if we fail to "stand fast in liberty wherein Christ hath set us free."

When God leads you to the edge of the cliff, trust Him fully and let go, only one or two things will happen, either He'll catch you when you fall or He'll teach you how to fly!

We must also remember that you have freedom of choice, but not freedom from choice. You must decide to walk with Christ or to walk alone.

A true disciple will desire to walk in the liberty of Christ and determine not to entangle himself again to bondage.